W9-AUD-954

PLAINFIELD PUBLIC LIBRARY DISTRICT

3 1907 00237 6027

PLAINFIELD PUBLIC LIBRARY
15025 S. Illinois Street
Plainfield, IL 60544

Let's Visit Italy

Susie Brooks

PLAINFIELD PUBLIC LIBRARY
15025 S. Illinois Street
Plainfield, IL 60544

PowerKiDS
press.

New York

Published in 2010 by The Rosen Publishing Group Inc.
29 East 21st Street, New York, NY 10010

Copyright © 2010 Wayland/
The Rosen Publishing Group, Inc.

All rights reserved. No part of this book
may be reproduced in any form without
permission from the publisher, except by
a reviewer.

First Edition

Library of Congress Cataloging-in-Publication Data

Brooks, Susie.
  Let's visit Italy / Susie Brooks.
     p. cm. -- (Around the world)
Includes index.
ISBN 978-1-4358-3029-5 (library binding)
ISBN 978-1-4358-8612-4 (paperback)
ISBN 978-1-4358-8613-1 (6-pack)
1. Italy--Description and travel--Juvenile literature.
2. Italy--Juvenile literature. I. Title.
DG417.B76 2010
914.504'93--dc22

                    2008051886

Manufactured in China

Note to parents and teachers
The projects and activities in this book
are designed to be completed by children.
However, we recommend adult supervision
at all times since the Publisher cannot be
held responsible for any injury caused
while completing the projects.

Web Sites
Due to the changing nature of Internet
links, PowerKids Press has developed
an online list of Web sites related to
the subject of this book. This site
is updated regularly. Please use this
link to access this list:
www.powerkidslinks.com/world/italy

Picture Credits
p6: © Walter Bibikow/JAI/Corbis; p7: © Wayland Picture Library; p8, title page: © Peter Adams/Getty; p9: © Heather Perry/National Geographic/Getty; p10: © travelstock44/Alamy; p11: © Wayland Picture Library; p12: © Travelpix Ltd; p13: © Richard Ross/Getty; p14: © Sergio Pitamitz/zefa/Corbis; p15: © UKraft/Alamy; p16: © Reuters/Corbis; p17: © Philip & Karen Smith/Lonely Planet Images/Getty; p18: © Vittoriano Rastelli/Corbis; p19: © De Agostini/Getty; p20: © Dennis Flaherty/Getty; p22: © Robert Harding Picture Library Ltd/Alamy; p23: © Wayland Picture Library; p24: © Chuck Pefley/Alamy; p25: © Pool/Immaginazione/Corbis; p26: © Zurab Kutsikidze/epa/Corbis; p27: © Schlegelmilch/Corbis; ©; p28: © John Slater/Corbis; p29: © Marco Bucco/Reuters/Corbis; Rita Storey/Wishlist; p31: © Wayland Picture Library.

Cover: The Leaning Tower of Pisa © Reuters/Corbis; Italian footballer Fabio Cannavaro (left) in a Euro 2008 qualifier against Georgia © Zurab Kutsikidze/epa/Corbis.

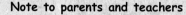

Contents

This is Italy!

It's easy to find Italy on a map because it is shaped like a boot! Italy is a country in southern Europe. Most people travel here by airplane.

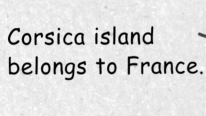

Corsica island belongs to France.

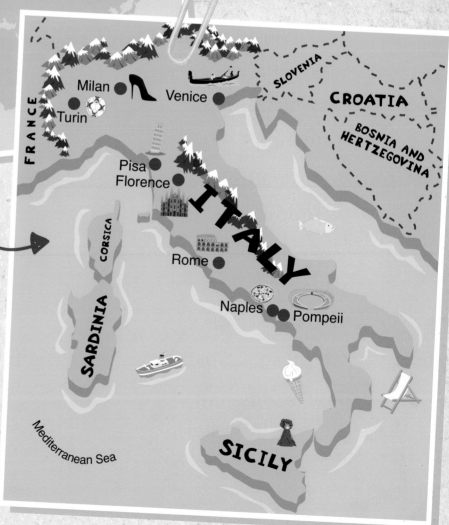

FRANCE

Milan
Turin

Venice

SLOVENIA

CROATIA

BOSNIA AND HERTZEGOVINA

Pisa
Florence

ITALY

CORSICA

Rome

SARDINIA

Naples
Pompeii

Mediterranean Sea

SICILY

The north and south of Italy are very different. But you'll notice things that are typically Italian, like the type of food and the language people speak.

This is the Piazza Navona, a square in Italy's capital city, Rome.

It was fun grabbing our suitcases from the conveyor belt at the airport.

Speak Italian!

good morning
buon giorno (bon-ji-**or**-no)

good afternoon
buona sera (bwon-a-**sair**-a)

goodbye
arrivederci (a-ree-vi-**dair**-chee)

Fun for all seasons

A lot of people travel to Italy for its summer sunshine. The weather can be very hot, especially in the south.

The island of Sicily is popular for beach vacations, even in the winter.

In September, we got soaked in a huge thunderstorm!

Weather in Rome

July—take sunscreen

October—take an umbrella!

Italy's mountains are cooler and wetter. People come skiing here in the winter snow. Spring and fall are good times for sightseeing.

Cycling trips are fun in the spring, but beware of the hills!

Be at home

This is the town of Positano on the Amalfi coast, southwest Italy.

Italy has many **resort** towns, built especially for **tourists** to stay in. There are also hotels in all the cities.

We stayed in a bed and breakfast— it was like being in someone's house!

You can make as much noise as you like in your own villa pool! This one is in the hilly region of **Tuscany**.

Some families rent vacation houses, called **villas**, in the countryside. If you're adventurous, you might prefer to camp.

Speak Italian!

bedroom
stanza (**stan**-za)

bathroom
bagno (**ban**-yo)

toilet
gabinetto (ga-bin-**ett**-o)

Winding travel

Cars, buses, and scooters make lots of traffic in Rome.

Driving around Italy is a good way to see the country—but the mountain roads can be very wiggly! There are tunnels through the Alps to other parts of Europe.

Speak Italian!

train
treno (**tre**-no)

bus
autobus (**out**-o-boos)

ticket
biglietto (bee-lee-**ett**-o)

Fast trains and highways take people from city to city. Some tourists hire scooters or motorcycles to travel around.

In the watery city of Venice, there are no cars but lots of boats.

We went on a **gondola** in Venice. The man rowing sang us songs.

Roaming in Rome

A visit to Rome is like traveling through time. The city was built by the Romans more than 2,000 years ago, but it has changed a lot since then.

People say if you drop a coin in the Trevi Fountain, you'll return to Rome some day!

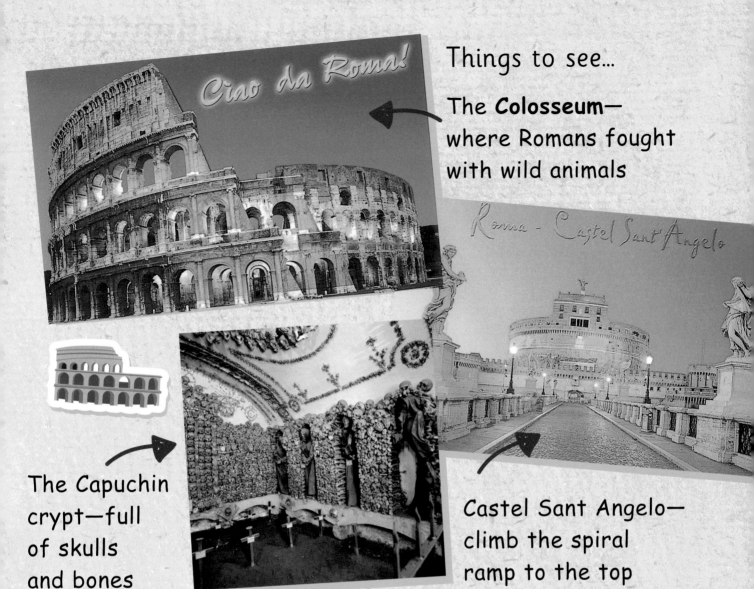

Things to see...

The **Colosseum**— where Romans fought with wild animals

Ciao da Roma!

Roma - Castel Sant'Angelo

The Capuchin crypt—full of skulls and bones

Castel Sant Angelo— climb the spiral ramp to the top

Be a Roman!

Take a day trip to Ostia Antica and...

- walk along a Roman street
- see ancient baths and toilets
- visit a Roman snack bar

13

City trips

You might stay in one of Italy's other great cities.

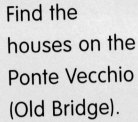

Find the houses on the Ponte Vecchio (Old Bridge).

Florence

Famous for: art and buildings
You can:
• climb the Campanile bell tower or the huge Duomo dome.
• pose next to **Michelangelo's** famous statue David.
• shop for gold on the Ponte Vecchio.

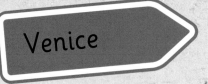
Venice

Famous for: canals and Carnivale
You can:
- explore secret streets by boat.
- feed pigeons in St. Mark's Square.
- watch glassblowers on Murano island.

Milan

Famous for: fashion and soccer
You can:
- see amazing inventions by **Leonardo da Vinci**.
- Take a day trip to Gardaland—Italy's top amusement park.

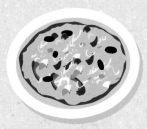

Look for strange-looking inventions at the National Museum of Science and Technology in Milan!

Naples—where pizza was invented
Turin—for winter sports and Fiat cars
Bologna—home of spaghetti bolognese

15

Special sights

These are some other places people like to visit in Italy.

North

- The Leaning Tower of Pisa —it hasn't fallen down yet!
- Cinque Terre ("five lands")— five cliff-top villages you can visit by boat

Fun sculpture parks

- The "monster garden" in Bomarzo near Rome
- Pinocchio Park in Collodi, Tuscany

• Pompeii—a town buried when a volcano, Mount Vesuvius, **erupted** almost 2,000 years ago. Now you can run around the ancient ruins!

• Matera—a mysterious place where people still live in prehistoric caves
• Capri—a magical island with a bright blue grotto

Vacation tip

You can see all of Italy's most famous sights in one mini-land at Italia in Miniatura near Rimini.

17

Wild Italy

People love to explore Italy's countryside. In the Alps, there are beautiful lakes and forests, where wolves and bears hide.

You might see a porcupine in the forests near Pisa.

I went up in a cable car in the mountains—it was scary looking down!

You can watch the Stromboli volcano erupting—from a safe distance!

Farther south, you'll see farmland and hills with villages perched at the top. Near Italy's "toe," there are islands with volcanoes.

Crops to look for

- Olives, for making oil
- Grapes, for making wine
- Wheat, for making pasta
- Oranges, lemons, and tomatoes

Buon apetito!

You have probably eaten Italian food—but it tastes better in Italy! Pizza, pasta, and ice cream were all invented here. Try as many different kinds as you can.

People say Italian ice cream (gelato) is the best in the world. It can be hard to choose the flavor you want!

Italian pasta is often topped with local cheeses, such as mozzarella and parmesan. Bread comes with each meal, so you can mop your plate clean!

Every pasta shape has its own name.

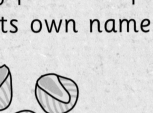

Vermicelli
"little worms"

Spaghetti
"little string"

Linguine
"little tongues"

Conchiglie
"shells"

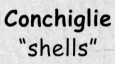

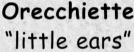

Orecchiette
"little ears"

Farfalle
"butterflies"

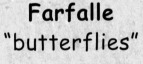

On the menu

risotto (ri-**zot**-to)
a creamy rice dish

gnocchi (n-**yock**-ee)
little dumplings
served in sauce

tiramisu (ti-ra-mee-**soo**)
a creamy coffee and
chocolate dessert

21

Go shopping!

You need to change your money to euros in Italy. Then you can buy **souvenirs** to take home. Look for things that remind you of your vacation.

Craft stalls like these are good for buying presents.

The Galleria in Milan has lots of shops and cafés.

Italians do most of their everyday shopping in small shops and markets. People on vacation in Italy buy a lot of leather and designer clothes.

Speak Italian!

please
per favore (pair-fa-**vor**-ay)

thank you
grazie (**grat**-zee-ay)

how much is it?
cuanto cuesta?
(cw-**an**-toh cw-**es**-ta?)

23

Italian life

There's a saying that goes, "When in Rome, do as the Romans do." If you do as the Italians do, you will probably stay up late and have fun with your family.

You might go to a restaurant for a treat in the evening!

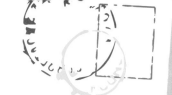

Special mail

Send a postcard from Vatican City! The **Pope** lives here—it is a separate country in Rome, with its own special stamps and post office.

Most Italians are **Roman Catholics**. Sundays are rest days when many stores close and some people go to church.

Crowds gather in the grounds of Vatican City to be blessed by the Pope.

At play

Going to a soccer game is an exciting way to join in Italian life. Italians are crazy about soccer! Most people back their local team.

Watch for the Italian team colors—they play in bright blue!

Other popular sports include basketball, cycling, and car racing. People from all over the world come skiing and snowboarding in the Alps mountains in the winter.

Italy is home of the Ferrari racing car.

I tried windsurfing at Lake Garda—I kept wobbling over and falling in!

Costume crazy!

If you like dressing up, go to Italy during Carnivale! This exciting festival marks the beginning of the Christian time of **Lent**.

People wear amazing masks at the Carnivale festival in Venice!

Different regions of Italy hold their own festivals at different times of year. A famous one is Il Palio, which happens in Siena in July and September.

Il Palio is a bareback horse race around the city square.

Famous fiestas

Easter Day for fantastic fireworks in Florence	Easter Monday for cheese-rolling races in Panecale	Epiphany (January 6) for presents from La Befana (the Italian female Santa!)	

Make it yourself

Make this Leaning Tower of Pizza to share with your friends!

You will need:

- long loaf of bread
- chopped tomatoes (canned)
- grated mozzarella cheese
- toppings—e.g. ham, mushrooms, green peppers, cheese—you choose!
- Italian herbs
- olive oil.

The Leaning Tower of Pizza

1. Ask an adult to cut the bread into slices about 1/2 in. (1 cm) thick.

2. Spread each slice with chopped tomatoes and cover with grated cheese.

3. Now add different toppings to each piece of bread—lay them in patterns if you like! Then sprinkle with Italian herbs and drizzle with olive oil.

4. Ask an adult to bake your mini-pizzas until they are crispy.

5. When the pizzas are out of the oven, allow them to cool for a minute. Then pile them up on a plate—and there's your Leaning Tower of Pizza!

Cheese + tomato = Margherita

Spinach + egg = Fiorentina

4 types of cheese = Quattro formaggi

TIP: Place the smallest piece of bread on top so it doesn't knock down your tower.

Useful words and further information

Colosseum	The ancient theater in Rome.
erupt	When a volcano throws out hot rock or ash.
gondola	A long, narrow boat found on the canals of Venice.
Lent	The 40 days leading up to Easter, when Christians traditionally give something up.
Leonardo da Vinci	A great Italian artist and inventor who lived from 1452-1519. His famous paintings include the Last Supper in Milan.
Michelangelo	A famous Italian artist who lived from 1475-1564. He painted the Sistine Chapel ceiling in Rome—it took him four years!
Pope	The leader of the Roman Catholic church.
resort	A place for vacationers with hotels and other facilities.
Roman Catholic	A type of Christian.
souvenir	Something you take home to remind you of somewhere you have been.
tourist	Someone who is on vacation or sightseeing.
Tuscany	A beautiful, hilly region in western Italy.
villa	A home in the countryside.

Books to read

Ciao Bambino!: A Child's Tour of Italy by Danna Troncatty Leahy (Authorhouse, 2004)

Countries Around the World: Italy by Kristin Thoennes (Capstone Press, 1999)

Italy ABCs: A Book About the People and Places of Italy by Katz Cooper (Picture Window Books, 2003)

Living in Italy by Ruth Thomson (Sea to Sea Publications, 2007)